TELL ME ABOUT
KINGS
AND QUEENS

D0921837

Acknowledgements

For permission to reproduce copyright material, the author and publishers gratefully acknowledge the following:
Cover: Camera Press   **Title page and back cover:** The Royal Collection © 2001, Her Majesty Queen Elizabeth II   **Top border:** Topham Picturepoint   **p.5** Topham Picturepoint   **p.6** (left) Topham Picturepoint (right) Topham Picturepoint   **p.7** With thanks to the Ironbridge Gorge Museum, Shropshire   **p.8** (left) Topham Picturepoint (right) Hulton Getty   **p.9** Topham Picturepoint   **p.10** Hulton Getty   **p.11** (left) Hulton Getty (right) Topham Picturepoint   **p.12** (main) J.S Library International (inset) Hulton Deutsch   **p.13** Topham Picturepoint   **p.14** Hulton Deutsch   **p.15** (left) Hulton Deutsch (right) Topham Picturepoint   **p.16** (main) Hulton Getty (inset) Topham Picturepoint   **p.17** The Royal Collection © 2001, Her Majesty Queen Elizabeth II   **p.18** Topham Picturepoint   **p.19** Corbis   **p.20** Topham Picturepoint

TELL ME ABOUT
KINGS
AND QUEENS

QUEEN
ELIZABETH II

written by
John Malam

Evans

Evans Brothers Limited

Contact the Author

Tell me what you think about this book.
Write to me at Evans Brothers.
Or e-mail me at: johnmalam@aol.com

Internet information

www.royal.gov.uk
The official website of the British
monarchy.

www.royalinsight.gov.uk/current/front.html
The official monthly guide to the life and
work of Britain's Royal Family.

www.royalresidences.com
Information about the Queen's royal
residences.

www.kirkdale113.freeserve.co.uk/queen.
htm
Hear the British national anthem, watch a
video clip of the Queen's coronation,
and read the text of the ceremony at this
site
www.goldenjubilee.gov.uk/content
The official Golden Jubilee website.

Published by Evans Brothers Limited
2A Portman Mansions
Chiltern Street
London W1U 6NR

© Evans Brothers Limited 2002

First published 2002

Printed in Hong Kong by Wing King Tong Co. Ltd.

All rights reserved. No part of this publication may be
reproduced, stored in a retrieval system, or transmitted, in any
form or by any means, electronic, mechanical, photocopying,
recording or otherwise, without prior permission of
Evans Brothers Limited.

British Library Cataloguing in Publication data.

Malam, John
    Tell me about Queen Elizabeth II
    1.Elizabeth, II, Queen of Great Britain 2.Queens - Great
    Britain - Biography - Juvenile literature 3.Great Britain -
    History - Elizabeth II, 1952 - Juvenile literature
    I.Title
    941'.085'092

ISBN 023752449X

Queen Elizabeth the Second is the world's most famous monarch. She is the head of the British Royal Family, and is known and loved by people all over the world.

When she was a young girl she did not expect to become the queen. But when something very unusual happened in the Royal Family, the little princess's life changed for ever. From then on, she knew that one day she would indeed be queen. This is her story.

The Queen's full title is: Elizabeth the Second, by the Grace of God, of the United Kingdom of Great Britain and Northern Ireland and Her Other Realms and Territories, Queen, Head of the Commonwealth, Defender of the Faith

On 21 April, 1926, a baby girl was born at number 17 Bruton Street, London. Her parents were the Duke and Duchess of York. The Duke's father – and the baby girl's grandfather – was King George the Fifth.

When she was five weeks old, the little girl was christened at Buckingham Palace, the King's London home. She was named Princess Elizabeth Alexandra Mary.

◄ Princess Elizabeth's parents, the Duke and Duchess of York

King George the Fifth, the grandfather of Princess Elizabeth ▼

Princess Elizabeth and her younger sister, Margaret. This tile picture was made for the Princess Elizabeth Children's Ward at Ealing Hospital in London.

When Princess Elizabeth was learning how to talk, she found it hard to say 'Elizabeth'. Instead, she said 'Lilibet'. Her parents liked to call her this name, but only in private.

When Elizabeth was four years old, her sister was born. Her name was Margaret Rose. Neither of the princesses went to school. Instead, a governess gave them English, French and history lessons at home.

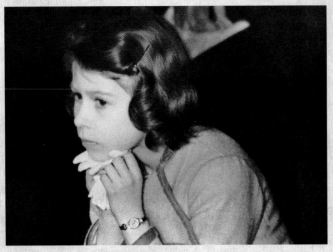

◀ Princess Elizabeth, aged 11

▼ King Edward the Eighth was king for only eleven months. He was Princess Elizabeth's uncle.

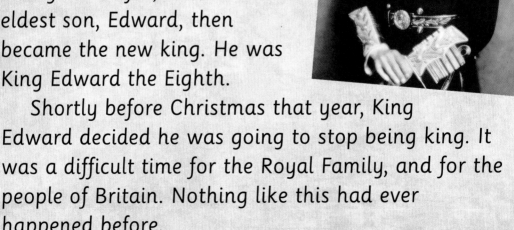

In 1936, when Princess Elizabeth was 10 years old, her life changed for ever. That January, her grandfather, King George the Fifth, died. His eldest son, Edward, then became the new king. He was King Edward the Eighth.

Shortly before Christmas that year, King Edward decided he was going to stop being king. It was a difficult time for the Royal Family, and for the people of Britain. Nothing like this had ever happened before.

Next in line to the throne was Princess Elizabeth's father, George. He had never expected to become king, but when his brother gave up the throne, George became the new monarch. He was King George the Sixth.

From then on, Princess Elizabeth, her parents and her sister, went to live in Buckingham Palace.

▲ King George the Sixth wearing his coronation clothes.

◀ Buckingham Palace, in London

Because Elizabeth was the elder of the two princesses, she knew that one day she would take over from her father as monarch. From the day her father became king, Elizabeth began to get ready for when she would be queen. She learned about Britain's past kings and queens and about the country's laws.

There was time for fun, too. Elizabeth learned how to ride, she went to the theatre, and she enjoyed swimming. When she was 11 she became a Girl Guide. Each week her Guide group met at Buckingham Palace.

Princess Elizabeth as a Girl Guide. She belonged to Kingfisher patrol.

As Princess Elizabeth grew older, she went with her parents on royal visits around Britain. These visits helped her to find out about the work she would do when she became queen.

When she was 13, Princess Elizabeth went to the Royal Naval College at Dartmouth in Kent. It was there that she met a distant relative of hers, a young man from the Royal Family of Greece. He was Prince Philip of Greece.

▲ Prince Philip as a young man. He would later become Elizabeth's husband.

◄ Elizabeth at Dartmouth College in 1939

In September 1939, Britain went to war against Germany. It was the start of the Second World War. The war years were a busy time for the young princess. As well as carrying on with her school lessons, she also did war work.

Princess Elizabeth joined ▶ the Auxiliary Territorial Service (ATS) near the end of the Second World War. The Army taught her how to drive.

▲ Windsor Castle, where Princess Elizabeth lived during the Second World War

The war ended in 1945. In 1947 Princess Elizabeth went with her parents and sister to South Africa. It was the first time she had been abroad.

After six months the Royal Family came home, and it was announced that Princess Elizabeth was going to be married. Her husband was to be Prince Philip of Greece. He was given a new title – the Duke of Edinburgh. They were married in November 1947.

Princess Elizabeth and the Duke of Edinburgh on their wedding day. They were given 2,428 wedding presents, which came from all over the world.

The following year Princess Elizabeth gave birth to a baby boy. He was named Charles. Two years later Princess Elizabeth had a baby girl, named Anne.

In 1952, King George the Sixth became very ill. He was too poorly to go on a visit to Kenya, in Africa, so Princess Elizabeth and Prince Philip went instead.

While the royal couple were in Kenya, King George died, and Princess Elizabeth immediately became Queen Elizabeth the Second.

Princess Elizabeth and Prince Philip with their first two children, Charles and Anne, in 1952

Preparations soon began for the Queen's coronation. Important people came from all over the world to watch the ceremony in Westminster Abbey, London, on Tuesday, 2 June 1953. At the end of the ceremony everyone in the Abbey called out:

"God save Queen Elizabeth.
Long live Queen Elizabeth,
May the Queen live for ever!"

▲ St Edward's, Crown, which has been used at every coronation since 1660

◀ The coronation of Queen Elizabeth the Second

15

People everywhere listened to the coronation ceremony on the radio. Some people were lucky enough to watch it on television, which was still quite a new invention.

Outside the Abbey millions of people lined the streets of London. They cheered and clapped as the Queen went by, riding in a golden carriage pulled by horses.

The coronation procession

Five months after her coronation, the Queen and the Duke of Edinburgh began the first of many overseas trips. They went to New Zealand and Australia, and to ten other countries that also had close links with Britain.

In 1960 the Queen had another baby, a boy named Andrew. Four years later, her youngest son, Edward, was born.

The official coronation portrait of Queen Elizabeth II

The Queen still leads a very busy life. Each year she makes hundreds of official visits, which can be to anywhere in the world. She has meetings with the British Prime Minister, and with leaders from foreign countries. Every day she is sent important news which tells her what the government is doing.

She is the head of Britain's Army, Navy and Air Force and supports more than 700 different charities and other organisations.

The Queen on a state visit to Ghana, in Africa, in 1999

The Trooping the Colour Parade celebrates the Queen's birthday. She used to ride in the parade on horseback, but today she sits on a chair whilst soldiers march past her.

All her life the Queen has liked animals, especially horses. She owns many racehorses, and likes to watch them race. She gives awards to people who have done good work – from sports players and business people to teachers and pop stars.

In 1977 the Queen's Silver Jubilee was celebrated, marking her first twenty-five years as monarch. Her Golden Jubilee, in 2002, celebrates her fiftieth year as Queen.

Queen Elizabeth the Second is one of the longest reigning queens in British history. But one day her reign will end. When it does, a new monarch will come to the throne, and a new coronation ceremony will be held.

Queen Elizabeth the Second and members of the Royal Family. She has four children and six grandchildren.

Important dates

1926 Princess Elizabeth was born in London

1936 Age 10 – her father became King George the Sixth

1939 Age 13 – she met Prince Philip of Greece

1945 Age 19 – she joined the Army

1947 Age 21 – she married Prince Philip

1948 Age 22 – her first child, Prince Charles, was born

1950 Age 24 – Princess Anne was born

1952 Age 25 – she became Queen Elizabeth the Second, when her father died

1953 Age 27 – her coronation

1960 Age 33 – Prince Andrew was born

1964 Age 37 – Prince Edward was born

1977 Age 51 – Silver Jubilee (25 years as queen)

1992 Age 66 – a fire damaged Windsor Castle

1993 Age 67 – Buckingham Palace was opened to tourists for the first time

1997 Age 71 – the Queen and the Duke of Edinburgh celebrated their Golden Wedding anniversary (married for 50 years)

2002 Age 76 – Golden Jubilee (50 years as queen)

Keywords

coronation
when a king or queen is crowned

governess
a teacher who teaches children at home

jubilee
a celebration

monarch
another name for a king or queen

reign
the time when a king or queen rules

throne
a special chair for a king or queen

Index